Frederick Douglass
Freedom Fighter

Kayla Roberts

Rosen Classroom™

New York

Published in 2014 by The Rosen Publishing Group, Inc.
29 East 21st Street, New York, NY 10010

Book Design: Jon D'Rozario

Photo Credits: Cover Stock Montage/Archive Photos/Getty Images; pp. 5, 9, 21, 22 (background) Leksus Tuss/Shutterstock.com; pp. 5 (Douglass), 13 Hulton Archive/Archive Photos/Getty Images; p. 7 SuperStock/SuperStock/Getty Images; p. 9 (Anna Murray) http://en.wikipedia.org/wiki/File:Anna_Murray-Douglass.jpg; p. 9 (Frederick Douglass) MIP/Archive Photos/Getty Images; p. 11 John Parrot/Stocktrek Images/Getty Images; p. 15 Buyenlarge/Archive Photos/Getty Images; p. 17 Courtesy of Library of Congress; p. 19 Zack Frank/Shutterstock.com; p. 21 jackkellerman/Shutterstock.com.

ISBN: 978-1-4777-2329-6
6-pack ISBN: 978-1-4777-2330-2

Manufactured in the United States of America

CPSIA Compliance Information: Batch #CS13RC: For further information contact Rosen Publishing, New York, New York at 1-800-237-9932.

Contents

Life as a Slave

Frederick Douglass was an African American who fought for freedom at a time when not everyone in the United States was free. In February of 1818, Frederick was born in Talbot County, Maryland. From the day he was born, he was a slave. This meant that he was "owned" by another person and was forced to work for them without being paid. Frederick spent his life fighting against slavery.

Slaves were often kept apart from their family. Frederick only lived with his grandmother when he was young.

In 1826, Frederick was sent to Baltimore, Maryland, to work for Hugh Auld, a ship **carpenter**. Hugh's wife, Sophia, taught Frederick to read and write. After he learned to read and write, Frederick discovered the abolitionist (aa-buh-LIH-shun-ihst) movement. This was a movement to end slavery.

In 1833, Frederick went to work for Hugh's brother, Thomas. Frederick tried to teach other slaves to read, but Thomas stopped him.

Frederick lived and worked near Chesapeake Bay in Maryland. He used to see the ships in the water and dream of being free.

The Journey to Freedom

Frederick wanted to escape from his life of slavery and become a free man. On September 3, 1838, he traveled from Maryland to New York to begin a new life of freedom.

Frederick got help on his **journey** from Anna Murray, a woman he fell in love with while he lived in Maryland. They were married on September 15, 1838, and had five children together.

Frederick had to change his last name in order to keep from being caught and sent back to his life as a slave. He chose Douglass as his new last name.

Anna Murray

Frederick Douglass

Speaking Against Slavery

After their wedding, Anna and Frederick moved to New Bedford, Massachusetts. In New Bedford, Frederick became an important part of the growing abolitionist movement.

Frederick began speaking at abolitionist meetings in New Bedford and became a very **popular** speaker. He spoke openly about his life as a slave. This showed people how bad slavery really was. His words **inspired** people to fight harder against slavery.

Frederick was one of the most famous abolitionists to ever live.

Frederick Douglass

Important Writings

Frederick gave many speeches about the abolitionist movement, and he also wrote about it. In 1845, he **published** his autobiography, which is a book he wrote about his own life. It was called *Narrative of the Life of Frederick Douglass, an American Slave, Written by Himself*. In the book, he wrote about his hard life in slavery and his escape to freedom. Frederick also published an abolitionist newspaper called the *North Star*.

Many people still read Frederick's autobiography today!

The Civil War

Frederick even helped President Abraham Lincoln during the Civil War. This war started in 1861 and was between two parts of the United States: the North and the South. The South wanted to have slaves, and it wanted to be its own country. The North fought to end slavery and keep the country together. Frederick helped to get African American **soldiers** to fight for the North.

Frederick met with President Lincoln during the war to help African American soldiers get better pay for their service.

Freedom for All

The North won the Civil War. After the war, the Constitution was amended, or changed, to end slavery forever. Thanks to the hard work of Frederick and other abolitionists, it became illegal for any American to own slaves on December 18, 1865.

The Constitution was also changed in 1870 to give all men the right to vote. Even men who had once been slaves could vote!

After 1870, voting on Election Day was open to all men, no matter what color their skin was!

Frederick didn't just fight for freedom for slaves. He fought for the rights of all people. He was an important part of the women's rights movement, too.

In 1848, Frederick was a part of the first women's rights convention in Seneca Falls, New York. He spoke about wanting women to have the right to vote. Frederick believed that all men and women in America should have that right.

These statues were made to honor the people who went to the first women's rights convention.

Frederick continued to fight for the rights of all Americans until his death on February 20, 1895. He's remembered as one of the most important members of the abolitionist movement. His words continue to inspire people today through his story about his brave escape from slavery. Frederick's life and work helped end slavery in America and helped make the country a better place.

Frederick Douglass was a brave freedom fighter whom we still honor today.

An Inspiring Life

1818 Frederick is born in February.

1826 Frederick is sent to work in Baltimore, where he learns to read and write.

1833 Frederick leaves Baltimore to work for Thomas Auld.

1838 Frederick escapes slavery and reaches New York City on September 3.

Frederick marries Anna Murray on September 15.

1845 Frederick's autobiography is published.

1848 The first women's rights convention is held in Seneca Falls, New York. Frederick speaks out for the right for women to vote.

1861 The Civil War begins.

1865 Slavery is made illegal in the United States on December 18.

1895 Frederick dies on February 20.

Glossary

carpenter (KAHR-puhn-tuhr) A person who builds or fixes things made of wood.

inspire (ihn-SPYR) To move someone to do great things.

journey (JUHR-nee) A long trip.

popular (PAH-pyuh-luhr) Well liked.

publish (PUH-blish) To print a written work in order to present it to the public.

soldier (SOHL-juhr) A person who fights in a war.

Index